12/24
£3

Grace Jones

A to Z

Smith Street Books

INTRODUCTION

Androgynous, otherworldly, restlessly creative; a power-suited powder keg with the ability to purr or put-down within the same breath, Grace Jones is undoubtedly one of a kind. A transformative performer, Jones went from 1960s drifter to 1970s supermodel and club disco queen, morphing into a new-wave, reggae and funk-dub revolutionary in the 1980s.

Escaping a harsh, repressively religious upbringing, Jones became a reactionary: glamourously kicking against society's norms and constraints; and speaking loudly about sexuality, racism, commercialism and pretence. As an artist, provocateur and musician she stands alone.

With regular creative partner Jean-Paul Goude – artist and iconic image-maker – and collaborations with the most respected fashion designers, photographers, set designers and milliners, Jones has been the centerpiece of some of the most startling and influential stage sets of all time. Experimenting with physical and musical form, Jones is synonymous with some of the most instantly recognisable photographs and album covers of all time. Draped in sculptural stagewear that references the intellectual avant-garde of the Ballets Russes and Dadaism, or powerfully subversive in leather, sporting a whip and a piercing stare, Jones has peerlessly blended fashion and high art, using her body – sometimes literally – as a canvas that transcends traditional ideas of beauty into something almost post-human.

Effortlessly blending chart success, slinky grooves and social commentary on tracks like 'Slave to the Rhythm', Jones helped create a new form of music in the early 80s when she fused her Jamaican upbringing and love of reggae with punk's obsession with dub and the burgeoning synthesiser scene. The result was a challenging but exciting musical form.

Through her quirky, surprising reworkings of other people's songs, she absorbed culture and returned it to the world passed through her own abstract filters. Throw in her penchant for outrage, her straight-down-the-barrel defiance and unwavering self-belief and you have the birth of a new sound and a 20th century icon.

Grace Jones remains an unflagging force of nature. Her fondness for champagne and oysters remains undiminished and, as a new generation seeks to emulate her creativity, bravado, abstraction, shock value and electrifying stage presence, Jones is still wowing the live crowds and showing the pretenders how it's done.

STEVE WIDE

A
is also for

Albums

Grace has, to date, released ten studio albums: *Portfolio* (1977), *Fame* (1978), *Muse* (1979), *Warm Leatherette* (1980), *Nightclubbing* (1981), *Living My Life* (1982), *Slave to the Rhythm* (1985), *Inside Story* (1986), *Bulletproof Heart* (1989) and *Hurricane* (2008).

...

Armani

In the late 70s, inspired by a trip to Japan and Akira Kurosawa's film *Kagemusha*, fashion designer Giorgio Armani created a collection based on what he called 'emblematic Japanese silhouettes', structures of armour and corsetry, which he entitled 'Samurai'. The collection made a strong impression on Jones, who ended up wearing one of the pieces for the iconic artwork on *Nightclubbing*.

...

Awards

Grace was nominated for a Grammy for Best Long-Form Music Video for *One Man Show* in 1983; three Best Supporting Actress Saturn Awards for *Conan the Destroyer* (1984), *A View to a Kill* (1985) and *Vamp* (1986). She was also nominated for a Worst Supporting Actress Razzie for 1987's *Siesta*.

...

Atila Altaunbay

Grace Jones married her former bodyguard Atila Altaunbay in 1996, but their relationship ended in 2004, allegedly after he held a knife to Grace's throat in a fit of jealous rage. Jones says in her memoir that they are technically still married because she hasn't been able to locate him in order to divorce him.

Jones has said, 'I won't cry. I am very male emotionally.'

In 1979, Jones' ex-partner Jean-Paul Goude told *People* magazine, 'Men think she's sexy. Women think she's a little masculine, so they're not jealous. Gays think she's a drag queen.'

Jones on her fluidity: 'I go feminine, I go masculine – I am both, actually. I think the male side is a bit stronger in me and I have to tone it down sometimes. I'm not like a normal woman, that's for sure...'

Jones connects the dual gender personality to her way of escaping a repressive religious upbringing. As a child she was beaten, often whipped, by her step-grandfather, a Pentecostal bishop called Mas P. This instilled in her a desire to be her own source of strength. Later she would reclaim the means of her abuse by incorporating whips into her stage shows, celebrating them as symbols of sexual power.

Jones has said that having both 'male' and 'female' personality traits has made her self-sufficient. 'I am my own sugar daddy. ... If I want a diamond necklace I can go and buy myself a diamond necklace.'

In her book *I'll Never Write My Memoirs*, co-written by Paul Morley, Jones describes herself as 'possessing two completely distinct selves'. She also describes her brother as 'church gay', a category she also applies to Prince. She used asexuality to conjure up, prophetically, a 'new gender'.

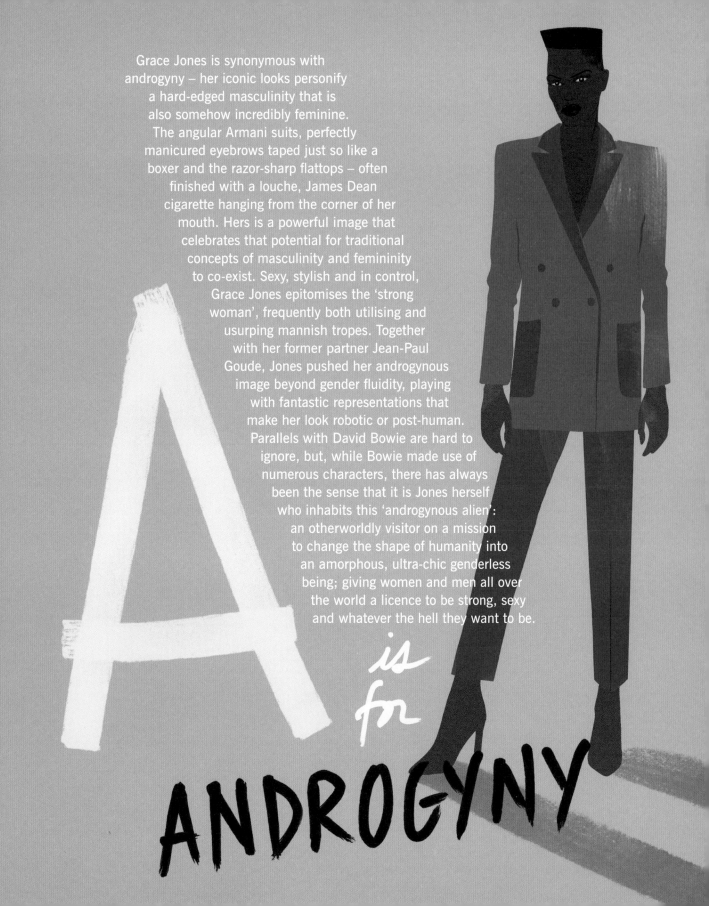

Grace Jones is synonymous with androgyny – her iconic looks personify a hard-edged masculinity that is also somehow incredibly feminine. The angular Armani suits, perfectly manicured eyebrows taped just so like a boxer and the razor-sharp flattops – often finished with a louche, James Dean cigarette hanging from the corner of her mouth. Hers is a powerful image that celebrates that potential for traditional concepts of masculinity and femininity to co-exist. Sexy, stylish and in control, Grace Jones epitomises the 'strong woman', frequently both utilising and usurping mannish tropes. Together with her former partner Jean-Paul Goude, Jones pushed her androgynous image beyond gender fluidity, playing with fantastic representations that make her look robotic or post-human. Parallels with David Bowie are hard to ignore, but, while Bowie made use of numerous characters, there has always been the sense that it is Jones herself who inhabits this 'androgynous alien': an otherworldly visitor on a mission to change the shape of humanity into an amorphous, ultra-chic genderless being; giving women and men all over the world a licence to be strong, sexy and whatever the hell they want to be.

A is for

ANDROGYNY

B is for BANNED

In 1998, at the tender age of 50, Jones was allegedly hit with a lifetime ban from Walt Disney World in Florida (some sources claim that she's been banned from all Disney properties) for flashing her breasts during a live performance. It certainly begs the question of why Disney would have hired Grace to perform in the first place since this is a pretty standard Jones onstage move (at Brooklyn's Afropunk festival in 2015, for example, she performed a legendary rendition of 'Slave to the Rhythm' hula-hooping topless for the duration of the song). Grace Jones has never been one to avoid controversy and appears to take enormous pleasure in pushing hard against the establishment. Throughout her career, Jones has continued to confront outdated gender, political, religious and social mores – she was never going to let the threat of her work being banned from broadcast or publication silence her.

Jones and Jean-Paul Goude's thrilling mid-80s Citroën CX 2 television spot is a striking piece of advertising, that was rumoured to have been banned in several countries.

The official reason is said to be because it promoted 'excessive speeding', although *IndieWire* made the suggestion that 'the strong, aggressive, literally larger than life image of a black woman, might have been just too much for some people to handle in 1985'.

Forget being banned, Grace is lucky she wasn't arrested when she tried to retrieve her then-errant boyfriend Dolph Lundgren from an LA hotel – with a gun. Grace said that in the climate of the time in LA, this behaviour seemed perfectly normal to her. Tom Holbrook, Dolph's manager, wouldn't let Grace see him. She describes herself as screaming through the locked hotel room door, 'I've got a gun! Let him out you bastard.'

Jones' hit 'Demolition Man' (from *Nightclubbing*) was written by Sting. While most people think the line, 'I'm a three-line whip / I'm the sort of thing they ban' is an S&M reference, in an interview with *Revolver* in 2000, Sting revealed the line's much less sexy inspiration, stating that, 'You have to know British constitutional law to know what it really means.' The Police would later record the song for their 1981 album *Ghost in the Machine*.

It was reported that pop megastars One Direction banned Jones from appearing with them on the same episode of *The Jonathan Ross Show*, for fear that they would be overshadowed by her and seem 'too tame' in comparison. While the band's representatives denied anything of the sort, there's no doubt that Grace would have stolen the show …

B is also for

Bloodlight and Bami
Director Sophie Fiennes (sister of actors Ralph and Joseph) made this 2017 documentary as an homage to Grace. It features live concert performances and intimate and rare footage of Jones. Fiennes told *The Hollywood Reporter*, 'The visually fetishised image of Grace isn't radically different from the person. She's someone who's kind of excessively alive.'

…

Boyfriends
Jones had a long relationship with designer and photographer Jean-Paul Goude. She was with producer Chris Stanley – although she denies the rumours that they were married – and she and actor Dolph Lundgren (her former bodyguard) were together for nearly five years. She dated Danish actor and strongman Sven-Ole Thorsen from 1990 (with whom she reportedly still has an open relationship). In 1996, she married her bodyguard Atila Altaunbay (she clearly has a type).

…

Guy Bourdin
Grace Jones was muse to the provocative French artist and fashion photographer. Known for pushing his models to (sometimes uncomfortable) extremes, Jones was well and truly on his wavelength – together they created some seriously over-the-top fashion moments.

…

Bulletproof Heart
Jones' ninth studio album was released in 1989 and would be her last for 19 years – until *Hurricane* in 2008. Nearly all of the material on *Bulletproof Heart* was co-written by Jones and then-boyfriend, musician and producer Chris Stanley. Three tracks were co-produced by C + C Music Factory.

C
is also for

Chic
Nile Rodgers told Vulture's Kera Bolonik that Grace Jones inspired Chic's song 'Le Freak'. Jones told him they could get in to Studio 54 by mentioning her name. Notorious Studio 54 doorman Marc Benecke denied them entry, 'the guy slams the door in our faces and tells us to fuck off … So we went to my apartment and started jamming on a groove, like "Aww … fuck off! Fuck Studio 54!" And it sounded great.' Realising they would never get the song on the radio, they changed the lyric to 'Ahhhh … freak out!', and a number one hit was born.

…

John Casablancas
The founder of Elite Model Management (and father of The Strokes' Julian Casablancas) apparently told Jones in the 70s that there was only room for one black model in his agency – who at the time was Beverly Johnson.

…

Compass Point All Stars
Island Records supremo Chris Blackwell pulled this A team together at Compass Point Studios in Nassau in the Bahamas in 1977. They worked with luminaries like Robert Palmer, Gwen Guthrie, Black Uhuru and Joe Cocker. After working on Grace Jones' LPs *Warm Leatherette* and *Nightclubbing*, they became her long-term backing band. The band included legends like Sly and Robbie, Wally Badarou, Wailers keyboard player Tyrone Downie, Marianne Faithfull's guitarist Barry Reynolds, percussionist Uzziah 'Sticky' Thompson and Mikey Chung who has played with Black Uhuru and Lee Perry.

…

Commercials
Jones appeared in commercial spots for Citröen, Honda Scooters, Sun Country Wine Coolers (!), and of course there was her famous spot for 'Strange' perfume in the movie *Boomerang*: 'It stinks so good!'

At the 2010 Royal Ascot, Jones revealed the source of her headwear obsession, 'My mum will tell you, we come from a church and everyone dresses up in hats.

We weren't even allowed to go into church without a hat, it was absolutely mandatory to wear a hat to church, so we feel naked without a hat. Thank God for that!'

Grace has her imitators of course, and the hooded cape was taken on most famously by Kylie Minogue in the video for 'Can't Get You Out of My Head', created by, appropriately enough, the British designer Mrs Jones (no relation).

Speaking to Bevy Smith during a radio interview on SiriusXM, Jones called out Treacy for recycling her looks with Lady Gaga, 'I know Philip needed to make some money, but you know what, can you just wait until I finish my tour before you repeat what we are working on?'

Grace has also enjoyed collaborations with namesake milliner Stephen Jones. His pieces for Grace have included a cowl complete with 'chic devil' mask, and an extraordinary woven wirework piece that torture-twisted its way around her torso.

At the London premiere of the documentary *Grace Jones: Bloodlight and Bami*, Grace slayed the red carpet in an enormous Treacy piece that can only be described as a cross between a funeral veil and a shrubbery.

C *is for* COWL

The draped cowl is one of Grace Jones' signature looks. Rendered in an array of colours, draped over the flattop and paired with a broad-shouldered cropped leather jacket and killer shades, or worked into a gown or bodysuit, the cowl has delivered some of Grace's most memorable fashion moments. In fact, the style has become so synonymous with her, you'll find countless patterns and articles devoted to knitting, sewing and draping in order to replicate the 'Grace Jones look'. But of course, the cowl is only the beginning when it comes to famous headgear. Grace can rock an outrageous hat like no one else, so it's no wonder she and fab Irish milliner Philip Treacy were drawn to each other. Treacy has created some serious head sculpture for Jones over the years, including a towering red lotus hat complete with stamen-like tendril, pieces that look part nun's hood–part warrior's helm, a sunburst of feather arrows and a Swarovski crystal–encrusted bowler hat that looks as though it's morphing into a disco ball.

D is for DISCO

The 70s were a good time for Grace Jones. She was a darling of the disco scene, and the clubs provided her with the perfect playground – a catwalk to strut her stuff and an arena to act out her fetishes. The Studio 54 photographs are infamous: Jones scorching hot in a batwing romper, casually accessorising a bare breast with a cocktail in hand; Jones at a New Year's party corralling a bevy of men who are on all fours and wearing nothing but bondage gear and dog collars; Jones and Divine hamming and glamming it up; Jones reclining like Cleopatra attended by a loincloth-clad slave; Jones snogging Dolph Lundgren. The New York disco was the place to see and be seen, and Jones' razor-edge cheekbones, lithe physique and bombastic style ensured that she outshone the dance floor lights and out-glittered the mirror balls. The disco sound itself was the perfect conduit for Jones. Up-tempo originals like 'I Need a Man' (co-written by Paul Adrian Slade and Pierre Papadiamandis) and mid-tempo discofied reworks of 'Send in the Clowns' and 'What I Did For love' from her debut LP *Portfolio* gained her voice the attention it needed. While the covers were a little on the naff side, 'I Need a Man' remains one of the classics of the disco era and propelled Jones into a career in music that would see her experiment more and more. Other disco hits followed – 'Do or Die' from *Fame* and the feminist anthem slash kinky innuendo classic 'On Your Knees' from *Muse*.

Jones' Paris nightclub of choice was a gay club called Club Sept. She described nights where she and her roommates – Jerry Hall and Jessica Lange, no less – would spend hours on their outfits. She said, 'When we dressed up we looked like nothing else … We had brazen appetites and desires.'

Jones described herself during the Studio 54 years as being, 'Lathered in foam and coke, tongued and flailed by drag queens, total strangers and horny hedonists, entertaining the creeps, freaks, strays, and lionized, living the un-American dream.' She said, 'I was the wildest party animal ever. I pushed myself to the limit and started from there.'

Disco is also the name of a CD box set released in 2015, featuring Jones' first three albums, all remastered plus bonus and live tracks.

Dance pioneer Tom Moulton produced Jones' first three LPs, *Portfolio*, *Fame* and *Muse*. Moulton is credited with essentially inventing the extended remix, the concept of the 12-inch single and the 'breakdown' – a section of the extended version of a track where all music except the drum beat drops out allowing the DJ to mix into another song.

In an article for *Electronic Beats*, Tim Lawrence views Grace Jones' disco days as a slightly clichéd process where Jones was finding her feet rather than discovering her true self. He goes as far as to say that the head of Island Records, Chris Blackwell, was 'all set to sign Jones based on her image'. Of the end of disco and the beginning of the 80s he said, 'Where other disco artists struggled to survive the backlash, Jones would relax into her mutant self.'

is also for

Dada

An avant-garde early 20th century art movement, Dada eschewed logic and the normal confines of art to create a dynamic movement of change. Created by artists like Marcel Duchamp and Hans Arp, it's no surprise that the absurdist nature of Dada appealed to the experimental Jones. Dadaist imagery sculpted her 80s look, and the Cabaret Voltaire and Ballets Russes greatly influenced the visuals and stage sets of her live shows. Jones said, 'I am disco, but I'm also dada.'

…

Divine

Paparazzo pioneer Ron Galella captured incredible photographs of drag queen, disco diva and John Waters' muse Divine celebrating Grace Jones' 30th birthday in 1978 at Xenon Disco. Jones had just released her second LP *Fame* and used her birthday party to launch the record. However, she was almost upstaged by the outrageous Divine. At one point Jones is seen feeding her birthday cake.

…

Dame Edna

In what must be the most perfect interview coupling ever, Grace Jones appeared on *The Dame Edna Experience* in 1989. An iconic Australian drag queen, Barry Humphries' outrageous character makes for the ultimate match for the rambunctious Jones, regularly reducing the singer to hysterics, particularly when Edna chides her other guest, Tony Curtis, for interrupting when she's trying to speak to Grace.

…

Deadly Vengeance

A 1981 blaxploitation film that, despite promoting itself as a 'Grace Jones film' only gives her around 10 minutes of screen time – and is all the worse for it.

E
is also for

Education

Grace attended Onondaga Community College in New York and majored in Spanish. She also studied theatre, and this took her to Philadelphia on a 'summer stock tour', where a troupe takes stage productions to other states. She stayed there, fully embracing the 1960s' counter-culture.

...

Brian Eno

Producer extraordinaire and musician Brian Eno was brought in to add a special flavour to Jones' 2008 comeback LP *Hurricane*. He played keyboards, added some vocals and produced some, though not all, of the tracks. He most notably played keyboards and produced the single 'Corporate Cannibal', one of the weirdest and darkest tracks Jones has ever produced.

...

Excercise

Jones' incredible physique is the result of some pretty hardcore exercise. At one time her exercise regime included working out twice a day with Arnold Schwarzenegger and Dolph Lundgren and boxing (culminating in her fitter-than-fit look on the cover of *Pull Up to the Bumper*). In more recent times Jones swears by hula-hooping.

...

'Evilmainya'

A little-known Jones track that was recorded for the soundtrack to 1992's *Freddie as F.R.O.7*, an animated parody of James Bond – about, you guessed it, a frog.

In a notorious and cringeworthy interview on Australian TV show *Day by Day* in 1985, Jones was told she came across as an 'aggressive lady'. She responded by saying, 'I think being aggressive in a positive way is very good.' When asked if she liked being masculine or feminine she said 'both' and when asked if that made her bisexual she calmly responded, 'It doesn't make me anything. I think it's ridiculous to categorise people for their feelings.'

In an episode of *Pitchfork's* interview series *Over/Under,* actress/singer Janelle Monáe spoke of Grace Jones' impact on her, 'She has redefined what is means to be a black woman in the entratainment industry. For me, she let me know that I can be as wild, as fearless, as free, as I want to be. Unapologetically.'

Jones has always embraced nudity and proudly flashed her breasts at photographers at the New York launch of her book *I'll Never Write My Memoirs*. To Jones, it's all part of liberation, an expression of sexual freedom.

Costume designer Zoe Koperski told *Vogue* that the harness uniforms in Pussy Riot's 'Make America Great Again' video were inspired by Grace Jones, and that they were used as a 'really strong symbol of empowerment'.

CAPITOL • Records

In her memoir, Grace denounces Capitiol Records for their treatment of her after trying to interfere with her creative vision, stating that had she been a man they would never have treated her with such little respect. 'It's why I want to fuck every man in the ass at least once. Every guy needs to be penetrated at least once … It's all about power.'

Grace on feminism: 'You have to own your power, it's that simple.'

E is for EMPOWERMENT

Grace Jones escaped a repressive and abusive religious upbringing to unleash upon the world a vision of strength and individuality. She's an icon of female and black empowerment. Throughout her career Jones has continually smashed barriers and perceptions about power, beauty, gender, desire, artistic expression and sexuality, always with a fierce glare and a sardonic smile, and above all, being entirely, unapologetically, 100 per cent herself. Grace's version of empowerment is all about ownership. She told *The Daily Beast*, 'That's what we say about empowerment: If you give up your power, you have no one to blame but yourself.' Unsurprisingly, Grace has no time for concerns that photographer and ex-boyfriend Jean-Paul Goude fetishised or exploited her image, describing their collaborations in a typically Jones way as, 'a visual description of an impossible original beast, only possibly from this planet, a voracious she-centaur emerging from an unknown abyss and confronting people's fears'.

F is for FAMILY

Grace Beverly Jones was born on 19 May 1948 (or 1952, depending on which sources you go by), in Spanish Town, Jamaica. Her parents were Marjorie Williams and Robert W Jones, a politician and clergyman. When Grace was young, the couple moved to Syracuse on America's East Coast to find work, leaving Grace and her brothers in the care of Marjorie's mother and her new husband Peart. Known to them as Mas P, their step-grandfather was a strict, religious disciplinarian who would beat or whip the children for the slightest infraction of the church's Draconian rules. This terrifying male authoritarianism would eventually be subverted by Grace to inform her own ferocious persona. When Jones' parents eventually settled in Lyncourt, New York – where Robert had established his own ministry, the Apostolic Church of Jesus Christ – the children, including thirteen-year-old Grace, finally joined them in the US. Jones has one child, Paulo, with long time collaborator Jean-Paul Goude. She has (arguably) been married twice, once to producer Chris Stanley and in 1996 she married one of her bodyguards, Atila Altaunbay (to whom she is apparently still technically married). Grace's father, Robert, died in 2008 and her mother passed away in 2017 at the age of 87.

Grace disputes that she was ever married to Chris Stanley, and maintains that he was murdered in Jamaica. She also says that she is still technically married to Atila Altaunbay, but she can't find him to divorce him.

Bishop Noel Jones, Grace's second brother, is the senior pastor of the City of Refuge church in Gardena, California, which has a congregation of over 17,000 people. The church has a choir whose debut album, *Welcome to the City*, hit number one on the Billboard Top Gospel Albums chart.

At the premiere of *Bloodlight and Bami* Grace devoted the 2017 documentary to her mother, saying 'I'm doing this for her.'

Grace's son, Paulo Goude, is part of the three-piece band Trybez who supported Grace on her *Hurricane* tour. Paulo has a daughter called Athena.

Jones has described her childhood as being 'crushed underneath the Bible'.

The song 'Williams' Blood' speaks of Grace's musical talent coming from her mother's side of the family. Born Marjorie Williams, Grace's mother had a lovely singing voice, and her father was a musician who played with Nat King Cole.

F

is also for

Fame
Grace Jones' *Fame* was her second album release. It came out in 1978 and was part two of her 'disco trilogy'. It was produced by Tom Moulton, who effectively sculpted her disco-era sound, and featured her classic 'Do or Die'. In the liner notes, Jones dedicated the album to Jean-Paul Goude. 'with love to a true Artist'.

...

Flattop
Stylist Christiaan Houtenbos, who lived in Jones' apartment block, created Grace's signature flattop. Houtenbos recounts that Jones stuck her head out of the window and shouted to him that she wanted a new haircut and Houtenbos used just a pair of scissors and a regular razor to create the perfect flattop.

...

Flash and the Pan
Iconic Australian songwriters Harry Vanda and George Young had created The Easybeats in the 60s and had a massive hit with 'Friday on My Mind', covered by David Bowie on *Pin Ups*. By the time the 70s came around, they had morphed into a new-wave outfit called Flash and the Pan, with two chart hits, 'Hey, St Peter' and 'Down Among the Dead Men'. Their track 'Walking in the Rain' from their first, self-titled LP, became one of Grace Jones signature tunes from her album *Nightclubbing*.

G

is also for

Gorillaz

Grace Jones appeared on the 2017 Gorillaz album, *Humanz*. The track, one of the standout numbers called 'Charger', features a full vocal from Jones, not just a sample. In an interview on SiriusXM, Damon Albarn revealed that he ran into Grace Jones at a nightclub, saying, 'I made the mistake of saying she looked like Little Red Riding Hood because she was wearing a red cape. She turned around and said "Little *Black* Riding Hood", and turned back. I didn't speak to her again.' Jones later enjoyed a performance of Albarn's *Monkey, Journey to the West* and Albarn was able to set up a collaboration. Apparently the recording took four hours and was made up of 90 different Grace Jones vocal samples. Albarn said of the session with Jones, 'It's slightly supernatural, her energy. Not entirely of this world.'

...

Paulo Goude

Jones' only child, fathered by Jean-Paul Goude, has followed in his mother's footsteps to become a model and musician. Also like his mother, he speaks fluent French. They often attend events together.

...

Galleries

The classic Robert Mapplethorpe photograph of Grace Jones covered in Keith Haring body paint, with the towering exotic headdress and conical bra, is jointly owned by The Tate and the National Gallery of Scotland. Artist Leonardo Montoya made a full head portrait of Grace Jones that hung in the Saatchi gallery. Saatchi was offering it for sale in 2018 with a seven-day money back guarantee for US$4770.

Goude stage-managed many of Jones' live shows and created many of her album covers. Together they created the icon we associate with Grace Jones – angular and abstract; transcending gender; part alien, part machine.

Grace described her collaboration with Goude as, 'This brutal, animalistic energy that was part disco, part theatre of cruelty, two lucid ways of presenting an appetite for life.'

Their personal relationship was not to last. Grace became pregnant with their son, Paulo, and Goude saw the writing on the wall. He said, 'I had no intention of staying with her. I wasn't happy with it.'

Many of Goude's images were manipulated, using a collage of multiple images in order to extend or exaggerate body parts or place limbs at impossible angles.

Jean-Paul Goude worshipped Grace, (or, at least, her image), 'She's the manifestation of all my fantasies. She's the face of the 80s.'

Goude said of Jones, 'I became jealous and possessive of the character that, through her, I was able to create, much more than the real person.' While Grace could not go on being treated merely as an object, 'It made me think that if I wasn't this perfect human being, it would not satisfy him.'

Goude's father was a French elevator repairman who married an American ballerina. His mother, who envied the athletic beauty of the black ballerinas she danced with, likely inspired Goude's obsessions.

is for

JEAN-PAUL GOUDE

Jean-Paul Goude was born in 1940 in Saint-Mande, France. A prolific photographer, film director, graphic designer and illustrator, he worked as art director for *Esquire* magazine during the 1970s. His professional and personal relationship with Grace Jones began during the disco scene in what both of them describe as 'around '77–78'. Still controversial, Goude's 1983 book *Jungle Fever* courts sexual and racial stereotypes, featuring hyper-stylised and manipulated images that have an undeniable sense of power. Goude infamously photographed Grace on all fours, caged like a wild animal; and Grace with a flattop in an angular Armani jacket (probably her most recognisable, and most gender-subverting picture). His image, used on 1985's *Island Life*, depicting Jones in an impossible arabesque, her skin polished to a high shine, is one of the most striking album covers of all time. While it's difficult not to see Goude's work as racist and exploitative (he told *People* in 1979, 'I had jungle fever … Blacks are the premise of my work.'), Grace herself sees the art differently, writing in her memoir, 'He transformed the story of my life into a series of visions and fantasies … It was collaborative, never him only doing me. I was not a model. I was a partner in design.'

KEITH HARING
is for

As two of the most innovative and edgy artists of the 20th century it makes sense that at some point Jones and pop artist Keith Haring would collaborate. Andy Warhol introduced them, and, as hedonists, they met frequently afterwards at nightclubs. Jones was a gay icon and defender of individuality; Haring was an outspoken gay artist. For Haring, Jones' body was the perfect canvas, and their famous 1984 18-hour marathon art session took place in photographer Robert Mapplethorpe's studio. Mapplethorpe was on hand to record the process, with Warhol in attendance to dispense wisdom and snap the occasional Polaroid for posterity. Haring and Jones continued to collaborate, working together on her live show at the much-loved gay club Paradise Garage, on her look from the 1986 film *Vamp*, and for the music video for 'I'm Not Perfect (But I'm Perfect for You)'.

Haring painted Jones' body for her role as Katrina the Vampire Queen in *Vamp* (1986). She performs an erotic dance routine using a Haring painted 'torso' chair as a prop.

In the film clip for 'I'm Not Perfect', Haring is shown sped up painting his designs on a 60-foot circle, before the eventual reveal of Grace on a podium wearing the towering black and white skirt.

Andy Warhol appears in the clip for 'I'm Not Perfect' saying, 'Grace is perfect.'

For the Mapplethorpe shoot, Grace wore a huge crown and rubber jewellery designed by David Spada.

The painting on Jones' back featured an abstract asexual figure with open arms.

According to Javier Porto, Mapplethorpe's assistant, there was some rivalry between Mapplethorpe and Warhol during the legendary 1984 shoot. Porto claims that Mapplethorpe requested Warhol not use a flash in his studio, preventing him from taking any decent photos of Jones.

is also for

Honda
Jones featured in commercials for Honda Scooters in 1986. One surreal ad pans up from rows of newborn babies to Jones saying, 'We all start out pretty much the same. But where do you go from there? It's entirely up to you.' Another ad with Adam Ant is a scream. Ant plays a shy boy, who's never 'ridden a scooter'. Grace seduces him saying, 'It's sexy!' He says, 'I'll take it.'

...

Trevor Horn
Legendary ZTT Records producer Trevor Horn can happily claim to be the person who helped put together what is probably Jones' most recognisable track. As co-writer and producer of the hit 'Slave to the Rhythm', and producer of the titular LP, Horn used his exemplary knowledge of 80s synthesisers and smooth production sounds to bring Grace Jones well and truly up to date.

...

Hurricane
Grace Jones tenth studio LP, released in 2008, was her first for 19 years. It features her son Paulo Goude on the track 'Sunset Sunrise', and the title track was co-written by Tricky. Brian Eno plays keyboards and adds vocals to 'Corporate Cannibal' (with Adam Green from The Mouldy Peaches) showing just how much of a cult icon Jones has become over the years. Prince's backing vocalists Wendy and Lisa add their skills to autobiographical track 'Williams' Blood'.

...

The Hunger Games
Grace Jones wrote the track 'Original Beast' for *The Hunger Games, Mockingjay Pt 1* soundtrack. Lorde curated the soundtrack and called Jones to ask her to contribute. Jones wrote the track with long-time collaborator Ivor Guest.

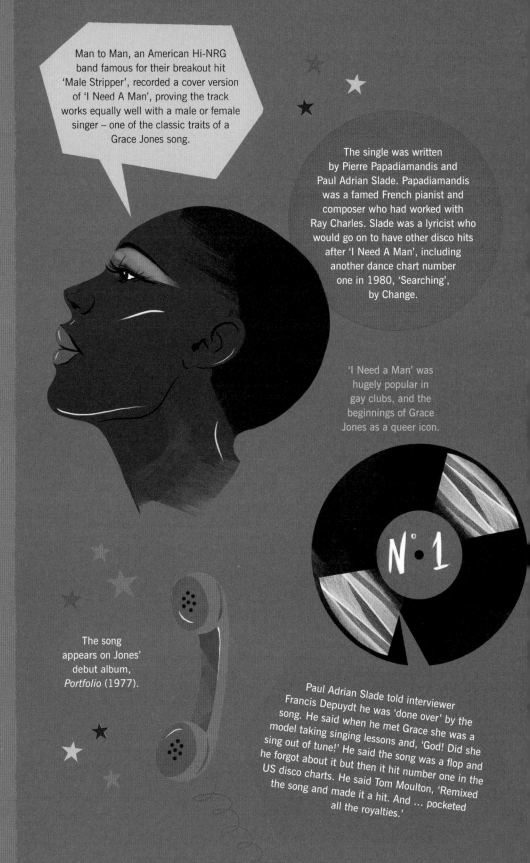

I
is also for

'I'm Not Perfect (But I'm Perfect for You)'
The first single from Grace's eighth studio album, *Inside Story*, was co-written by Bruce Woolley and produced by Nile Rodgers. Grace Jones has said that the song was the result of some flirting and banter with Mick Jagger, where they ended up discussing the pitfalls of being in a relationship as a famous person. Apparently the two of them came up with the line, 'I'm not perfect, but I'm perfect for you' together, but Jagger never asked for credit.

...

In Living Color
'Do you find me sexayyyyyyyy?' *In Living Color* was an American sketch show that launched the careers of Jim Carrey and Keenen Ivory Wayans and featured many of Wayans' extended family in the cast. Kim Wayans' portrayal of Grace Jones as the blind date of the hapless Keenan is hilarious. 'Would you like a piece of my tail, Harvey?'

...

Island Life
The Grace Jones compilation album from 1985 sums up her career to that point and remains one of her best-selling records. The Australian version came with a blue vinyl bonus disc of 12'' remixes. Jean-Paul Goude's classic cover image has been imitated by many but never matched.

...

Imitators
Rihanna imitated Jones' Keith Haring look in her 'Rude Boy' clip, and Kylie's cowl in her 'Can't Get You Out of My Head' video was a direct homage to the famous Jones headgear. Nicki Minaj and Amber Rose have both borrowed from Jean-Paul Goude's image of Jones as a caged animal. And Lady Gaga's entire schtick seems to be trying to *be* Grace – a fact that Jones is not very impressed by.

Man to Man, an American Hi-NRG band famous for their breakout hit 'Male Stripper', recorded a cover version of 'I Need A Man', proving the track works equally well with a male or female singer – one of the classic traits of a Grace Jones song.

The single was written by Pierre Papadiamandis and Paul Adrian Slade. Papadiamandis was a famed French pianist and composer who had worked with Ray Charles. Slade was a lyricist who would go on to have other disco hits after 'I Need A Man', including another dance chart number one in 1980, 'Searching', by Change.

'I Need a Man' was hugely popular in gay clubs, and the beginnings of Grace Jones as a queer icon.

N°1

The song appears on Jones' debut album, *Portfolio* (1977).

Paul Adrian Slade told interviewer Francis Depuydt he was 'done over' by the song. He said when he met Grace she was a model taking singing lessons and, 'God! Did she sing out of tune!' He said the song was a flop and he forgot about it but then it hit number one in the US disco charts. He said Tom Moulton, 'Remixed the song and made it a hit. And … pocketed all the royalties.'

I
is for
I NEED A MAN

Grace Jones' 1975 debut single was the perfect song for the disco diva's launch into music stardom. Jones was still working regularly as a high fashion model at the time and her catwalk moves and reputation as a carousing night owl gave the single the impetus it needed. It was perfect for Jones – an almost predatory song about female lust, empowering and entertaining, sexy, driven and vulnerable. The original version of the track came out on lesser-known disco label Orfeus in France, where Jones was living and doing most of her work. The American dance label Beam Junction picked it up, and it aroused interest but failed to trouble the charts. But Jones' signing to Island Records in 1977 saw the single remixed and re-released. The track reached number one on the Billboard dance chart (83 on the regular chart), not a full-blown hit, but enough to kick off part one of the Grace Jones music career.

J is for

Although she moved to the US when she was 13, Grace Jones never lost her connection to her home country, Jamaica, and her birthplace, Spanish Town. Jones clearly has mixed feelings about her early life in Jamaica, suffering under a conservative, highly religious father and then step-grandfather whose dictatorial control has been frequently described by Jones as 'abusive'. Sophie Fiennes' 2017 documentary *Grace Jones: Bloodlight and Bami* sees Jones return to her home country, talking to local residents, gathering with family and friends and swimming in a lake in a tranquil scene that shows that despite her upbringing, she retains some fond memories and deep affection for Jamaica. Certainly reggae greatly influenced her sound, especially in the early 80s where she redefined the form. She returned to Jamaica to her then-boyfriend Chris Stanley's Music Mountain Studio in the late 80s to record *Bulletproof Heart*. Jones also worked extensively with Jamaican musicians like Sly and Robbie.

JAMAICA

Grace wore an eye-popping costume as part of her Hammerstein Ballroom set in New York in 2009, a butt-baring beaded ensemble in Rastafarian colours.

The poverty of Jamaica is there for all to see in *Bloodlight and Bami*, when Jones pays a visit to childhood neighbour Miss Myrtle. Myrtle ironically says, 'Welcome to my palace,' on showing Jones her dilapidated quarters. Jones credits Miss Myrtle with, 'saving her from regular floggings,' and describes her as, 'A woman who sashayed along the road, swinging her arm like a queen.'

Jones has said, 'Growing up in Jamaica, the Pentecostal church wasn't that fiery thing you might think. It was very British, very proper. Hymns. No dancing. Very quiet. Very fundamental.'

Jamaica

Jamaica has appeared sparsely in Jones' work, referenced in particular in songs like 'My Jamaican Guy' and on the compilation title Island Life (also a reference to the Island Records label – a fitting label for Jones as it was founded in Jamaica).

J *is also for*

Jungle Fever
Jean-Paul Goude's controversial photographic art book was released in 1982. The title implies a white male obsession with exotic women and the pictures confirm it – the cover famously shows Jones on all-fours in a cage, naked and snarling like a wild animal. Other iconic pictures of Grace included in the book are those that would go on to be the album covers for *Nightclubbing*, *Slave to the Rhythm* and the anatomically adjusted image that was used on the cover of *Island Life*. The book doesn't only feature Grace, though. Goude's other subjects include David Bowie, Russ Tamblyn (Dr Jacoby from *Twin Peaks*), Sabu (the wrestler) and Kellie the Evangelist Stripper (Kellie Everts, the one-and-only 'Stripper for God').

...

'Jones the Rhythm'
'Jones the Rhythm' was the second single released from the concept album *Slave to the Rhythm*. More upbeat and rock-inspired than the album's famous title track 'Jones the Rhythm' features the Ambrosian Singers, a famous London choral group, as well as actor Ian McShane reciting passages from Jean-Paul Goude's *Jungle Fever*. The song's release was downplayed, almost as an afterthought, and it didn't trouble the charts. As it was essentially a remix of 'Slave to the Rhythm' (as was everything on the album), it served more as a promotional release. In its own remixed format it appeared as the song 'G.I. Blues' on the B-side of *Slave to the Rhythm*.

...

Joy Division
Ahead of her time, Jones is said to be the first artist to release a Joy Division cover. She covered the track 'She's Lost Control' as a B-side for the single 'Private Life', from the album *Warm Leatherette*.

K

is also for

Kenzo

Grace Jones regularly modelled for fashion designer Kenzo Takada during the 70s. Their most famous collaboration was at Studio 54 in 1977. At the 2016 launch of her book, *I'll Never Write My Memoirs*, at Le Bon Marche in Paris, many fans lined up to get their book signed. Among them was Kenzo. He told *WWD*, 'We had a blast together. I saw her walking an Issey Miyake show. She was stunning. I asked her to walk for me. She was wearing a men's suit, and had her brush hair cut. It was unexpected, modern and poetic.' He described her as, 'Loyal and simple.'

...

Katrina

Grace Jones' character in the 1986 film *Vamp* was an OTT, ultra-stylized vampire stripper. Her look was apparently based on Pris from *Blade Runner* – bewigged with heavy make-up. Her stripper dance scene is the highlight of the film.

...

Kissing

Grace Jones' notorious screen (and photographic) kisses included Alan Carr, Rosie Perez, Emilie De Ravin, and Roger Moore and Christopher Walken in *A View to a Kill*. Of these, the most notorious was Alan Carr. Jones snogged the *Chatty Man* talk show host, rendering him 'unchatty' for the first time ever. (At least he didn't get slapped like Russell Harty!) Carr later said that Jones had been drinking champagne, and he described her as 'drunk and horny'.

...

Knickers

At the 2012 *GQ* Men of the Year awards Grace Jones presented the 'Legend' award to Tom Jones. Tom Jones quipped 'It's great to be in London. But at 72, it's great to be anywhere.' Grace Jones upstaged him by giving him a pair of her knickers. She said, 'It was difficult getting them over the heels.'

Jones' version of 'Do or Die' refers to her star sign, Taurus, and being born on the 19th of May. As Kitt was born on January 17, her version changes the lyric to fit her star sign, Aquarius. However, Kitt applies a little artistic license for the sake of a rhyme, singing 'I was born on New Year's Day'. The star sign for January 1 is Capricorn.

In 1953 Eartha Kitt recorded a version of the French standard 'C'est Si Bon'. Jones would later record French standards 'La Vie en Rose' and 'Les Feuilles Morte'. Both 'C'est Si Bon' and 'Les Feuilles Morte', were songs made popular in France by Yves Montand.

Kitt played Catwoman as a prowling, purring, slinky villain. It's not a giant leap to imagine Jones playing the part in a very similar way, especially as there was tight leather involved.

Kitt appeared with Jones alongside Eddie Murphy in the film *Boomerang*. Jones was seriously out there as the model Helen Strangé, an over-the-top parody of herself that she took to with gusto. Not to be outdone, Kitt played Lady Eloise, who seduces a younger Eddie Murphy in a scene that will forever change the way you think about asparagus.

Orson Welles once described Kitt as, 'The most exciting woman on earth.' Jones claims that Welles once told her on a talk show, 'Most performers seduce an audience. Grace, you rape an audience,' but that he meant it 'in a good way'.

K is for EARTHA KITT

Eartha Kitt recorded a cover of Jones' 1978 song 'Do or Die,' for her 1989 album *I'm Still Here*. Kitt was a singer, actor, dancer and comedian whose career spanned almost 55 years. With an extremely distinctive vocal style, a tendency to speak her mind and defiantly open about sexuality, it's hard not to see Kitt as something of a kindred spirit to Jones. Born in 1927 and hailing from humble cotton-farming origins, Kitt would go on to break from poverty and rise to international stardom. Less experimental than Jones, Kitt was nonetheless a firebrand in her day and challenged many social norms. As Kitt herself says, 'The price we pay for being ourselves is worth it.' Grace Jones would later express similar sentiments, saying, 'I've always been a rebel. I never do things the way they're supposed to be done … regardless of what the rules are or what society says.'

L is for DOLPH LUNDGREN

Towering six-foot-five-inch hunk of Swedish he-man Dolph Lundgren powered to fame in 1985, after playing the rock solid, immovable Ivan Drago in *Rocky IV* opposite Sylvester Stallone. A high achiever, Lundgren was winning European and Australian karate championships while earning his master's degree in chemical engineering at the University of Sydney. Lundgren was preparing to move to Boston (as he had been offered a Fulbright scholarship to MIT) and earning a living as a bouncer in Sydney's Kings Cross when Grace Jones spotted him. She hired him as her bodyguard and the two soon became lovers. After just two weeks at MIT, Jones talked Lundgren into the bright lights of Manhattan, where he briefly worked as a model and as a bouncer at The Limelight (where he was reportedly fired for eating a sandwich in the stairwell). She then nabbed him a small role in *A View to a Kill* where he played a KGB henchman (who could easily have taken out Roger Moore's James Bond but the two never got to square off) leading to the role in Rocky IV that rocketed him to stardom. Jones and Lundgren dated for four years, but their relationship became strained as Lundgren's fame and success increased, and notoriously ended with Grace Jones trying to fetch him from a hotel in LA with a loaded gun.

In *I'll Never Write My Memoirs*, Jones describes the scene at the hotel, 'It was as though Tom [Holbrook, Dolph's manager] was holding him hostage and we had come to rescue him, hair flying, legs flailing, breasts heaving, guns flashing, music pumping.'

Lundgren describes a time before he left MIT in Boston, when he arrived on campus on a motorbike with Jones, both clad head to toe in leather.

Jones said of the gun incident, 'In one of the many lives I never got to live, another Grace shot Dolph there and then... And that was the end of the ballad of Grace and Dolph.' She settled for cutting up his clothes and throwing them in the fireplace instead. Despite this, Jones says that they have remained friends.

Jones and Lundgren did a memorable, full and partially nude photo-shoot for *Playboy* magazine in July 1985. The striking portraits were taken by Helmut Newton.

'La Vie en Rose'
The third single from her first LP, *Portfolio*, 'La Vie en Rose' is the track that really kicked off Jones' music career. A cover of the Edith Piaf classic, Jones added a bossa nova beat and a touch of swagger, and made the song her own.

...

'Love is the Drug'
The Roxy Music classic was released by Jones as the second single from her 1980 LP, *Warm Leatherette*. Considering Ferry's song was a huge hit for Roxy Music, reaching number two in the UK, it's surprising that Jones' version didn't chart on first release. Nonetheless it remains one of her most popular live tracks.

...

Lady Gaga
A huge Jones fan, Lady Gaga was desperate to work with her. Gaga said, 'There's nobody I love more than Grace Jones. She's like my personal Jesus.' Jones said no to the collaboration crushingly saying that Gaga was soulless, and that she'd prefer to work with 'someone who is more original and someone who is not copying me'. Ouch.

...

Lil' Kim
Jones guested on the Lil' Kim track 'Revolution', from her 2000 LP *The Notorious K.I.M.* The track contained a sample of The Notorious B.I.G.'s 'Hypnotize', and also featured Lil' Cease (Biggie's cousin) from hip hop group Junior M.A.F.I.A.

...

Karl Lagerfeld
Partying with, and walking catwalks for, designer Karl Lagerfeld was a regular 80s pasttime for Jones. But their most iconic moment came when Jones wore the Lagerfeld-designed leather space ninja outfit and 'basket' hat to the 1983 Grammys. Jones chose it because she thought it looked like a 'winner's outfit'. She lost to Duran Duran.

M is also for

'My Jamaican Guy'
The third single released from the 1982 LP *Living My Life*, 'My Jamaican Guy' wasn't a smash hit, but went on to become one of Jones' signature tunes and featured a truly iconic cover image – Grace with the thin bone through her nose lining up perfectly with her flattop. Grace Jones admitted in her memoir that the song was written about Tyrone Downie from Bob Marley's band The Wailers, who she had a mad crush on. She said he 'was with somebody else. He was a beautiful guy. He doesn't even know I wrote it about him.'

...

Roger Moore
Allegedly, during the filming of *A View to a Kill*, Jones and Moore didn't get along. Jones has said that Moore once asked her to stop looking at him with 'such venom'. Despite this, Jones has also described Moore as being a big 'softie' with 'incredibly hard legs and the stiffest hair'. When Moore passed away in 2017, Jones told *The Hollywood Reporter*, 'Roger will stay in my memory forever as a great gentleman and great father. He will always remain one of my best experiences in my filming career.'

...

Modelling
Grace Jones said that modelling agencies in America were too narrow-minded and didn't understand her at first. She had to go to Paris, where she found them to be more accepting. She told Andy Warhol in *Interview* magazine, 'In three months I was on four covers. My timing was just right ... They went wild.'

...

Mendoza
People often think that Grace Jones' real surname is Mendoza, but Jones claims that it was an alias she used in order to keep things from her parents when she was in her twenties.

In *A View to a Kill*, Jones' May Day executes a dramatic dive off the top of the Eiffel Tower, parachuting to safety.

In an interview with CNN's Christiane Amanpour, Jones described being told to meet the producer of *Gordon's War* at his house, '... he poured some champagne. He was in his bathrobe. He took me to a room, of course I didn't know his house, and it was his bedroom. So with the champagne ... I splashed it in his face and walked out the door.'

According to her memoir, Jones was offered the lead part in *Blade Runner* in 1981 but turned it down without reading the script because then-boyfriend Jean Paul Goude was feuding with Ridley Scott. Jones said she read the script not long after and called back to say yes to the part because she loved it so much, but by then it was too late. The styling of Grace Jones' character Katrina in *Vamp* was said to be based on Daryl Hannah's Pris in *Blade Runner*.

1987's star-studded and surreal *Siesta* was one of Jones' smaller roles but still sees her very memorably greeting Julian Sands' character by pulling a real rat from her hat, purring, 'Meet Roscoe.' While brief, the role made enough of an impression to earn her a Razzie nomination for Worst Supporting Actress.

Boomerang director Reginald Hudlin recalled that there were so many comedians on set that the shoot was constantly hilarious, adding, 'What Grace was doing on the set while we were shooting was so funny that I remember Halle (Berry) crying off camera, cause she was trying to keep a straight face but she couldn't. So whenever she was off-camera, she would just be literally crying because she was laughing so hard.'

M

is for

MOVIES

Not content with owning the catwalk and the dance floor, Grace Jones is equally legendary for her iconic film performances. She first hit the big screen in the Ossie Davis action flick *Gordon's War*, playing Mary, a drug mule. It was a small part, but her screen presence was undeniable. Her breakout role came 11 years later as Zula in *Conan The Destroyer*, soon followed by badass Bond girl/villain May Day in *A View to a Kill* – a role many agree is the one bright spot in one of the franchise's weakest offerings. This set Jones up for a career path of memorable, scene-stealing turns in otherwise fairly unmemorable films, the most successful being the 1992 Eddie Murphy hit *Boomerang*.

N is for NIGHTCLUBBING

Despite having four popular albums under her belt by 1981, it was *Nightclubbing* that propelled Grace Jones into superstardom. Island Records founder Chris Blackwell had become intrigued with Jones and he assembled a crack team of musicians and producers to help her make 1980's *Warm Leatherette*, while allowing her to develop her own style and ideas. The recording of *Nightclubbing* came together at Compass Point Studios in Nassau in the Bahamas and the assembled backing crew became known as the Compass Point All Stars. For the *Nightclubbing* sessions, the All Stars consisted of the bass and drum combo of Sly and Robbie, keyboardist Wally Badarou, guitarists Barry Reynolds and Mikey Chung and percussionist Uzziah 'Sticky' Thompson. Sly and Robbie had been listening to new forms of dance music, and Blackwell was a fan of Black Uhuru's 1980 mechanical reggae album *Sensemilla*. Influences from Bowie and Kraftwerk completed the transition of Jones' sound and, fuelled by ideas forged on *Warm Leatherette*, a kind of new-wave art-pop funk was born.

Nightclubbing went top 10 in five countries including number two in Holland and number five in Australia. It was Jones' highest mainstream US Billboard chart placement to date, reaching 32.

The album featured some choice covers. Bowie and Iggy Pop's 'Nightclubbing' was the first track recorded and was perfect for Jones' aloof, androgynous élan. Vander and Young's 'Walking in the Rain' and the Police's 'Demolition Man' made for some exhilarating robo-funk.

A previously unreleased track from the *Nightclubbing* sessions adds another brushstroke to the overall picture. It's not hard to draw comparisons between Grace Jones and Gary Numan, and her version of Tubeway Army's 'Me! I Disconnect From You' is as wonderful as it is unexpected. Jones swapped Numan's frosty, lamenting synth crunch for a sinister funked-up Latino groove, creating something altogether different.

The *Nightclubbing* LP is one of music's all-time standout album covers. The image is a painted photograph by Jean Paul Goude showing Jones in a razor-sharp Armani suit, a flattop that would have the bubble dead centre on a spirit level and a defiant glare that would make a bear think twice before attacking. Topped off with a hanging, unlit cigarette channelling Hollywood rebels like James Dean. Together Goude and Jones managed to make an image that was both classic and futurist, the perfect accompaniment to *Nightclubbing*'s musical style.

N *is also for*

Jack Nicholson
In *I'll Never Write My Memoirs*, Jones recounts 'turning down' Jack Nicholson during her modelling days. The two met while Nicholson was promoting *One Flew Over the Cuckoo's Nest* in Japan and Jones recalls that, while the other models were starstruck and 'throwing themselves at Jack', Jones 'caught his eye' and 'could tell what he was up to. I wagged my finger. *No, Jack. No way*.'

...

The Normal
The UK minimal electronic outfit helmed by Daniel Miller wrote the original version of 'Warm Leatherette' in 1977. Jones covered it in 1980 and even named her LP after the song.

...

Gary Numan
Jones' cover of the Gary Numan song 'Me! I Disconnect From You' – the opening track of the Tubeway Army album *Replicas* (well known for featuring the often-covered 'Are Friends Electric?') – was recorded for Jones' 1981 LP *Nightclubbing* but was curiously left off the record. The track was finally released on the 2014 expanded reissue of the album.

...

Necklace of bones
While modelling in Paris, Jones turned up to a party hosted by French politicians completely naked except for a necklace made of bones. When asked about it later she said, 'It was no big deal.'

...

Nefertiti
While performing at Studio 54 in 1977, Jones styled herself as Nefertiti, the wealthy Egyptian queen from 1300 BC. She was 'waited on', by a group of near-naked male dancers with heavy eye make-up and loincloths.

O

is also for

Opera

Opera legend Luciano Pavarotti held a benefit concert for Angolan refugees in 2002 in his hometown of Modena, Italy. The *Pavarotti & Friends* benefit gig included Lou Reed, James Brown, Andrea Bocelli, Sting … and Grace Jones. While the 'friends' usually contribute to their duets in their own musical style, Jones instead decided to match Pavarotti's operatic delivery – to astonishing effect. While she left much of the vocal heavy lifting to Pavarotti, Jones put in an incredible performance, imbuing the song with a dark and powerful atmosphere.

…

Oyster shot

During Grace's 2010 appearance on *Alan Carr: Chatty Man*, she encourages Carr to try an oyster. Seeing him gag, she convinces him to spit it out directly into her gloved hand. Jones appeared again on the show in 2015, convincing Carr this time on an oyster and limoncello shot. He enjoys it about as much as the first one, but cheers up considerably when Jones licks his face clean.

…

Opera de Paris

Jones once made a spectacular entrance to the l'Opera de Paris, arriving to great applause in a slinky purple hooded sheath dress with Dolph Lundgren on her arm. She performed 'La Vie en Rose' on the grand staircase, almost outshining the stunning building itself.

…

'On Your Knees'

The only single to be released worldwide from Jones' third LP, 1977's *Muse*, 'One Your Knees' reached a respectable 28 on the US Dance chart. In some territories the track was released as a double A-side with 'Don't Mess with the Messer'.

Of losing the Grammy to Duran Duran, Jones said it was, 'Enough to make me scream and scream.' She would later guest on the Arcadia (Duran Duran side project) single 'Election Day', showing all was forgiven.

During 'Feel Up', Grace appears like a wind-up musical toy, drumming mechanically in an enormous red halfmoon hat. Her one man show expands to three Graces, then five, then seven.

A One Man Show was beaten by Duran Duran's self-titled video for the Grammy. Grace wrote in her memoir that they said to her, 'Oh, Grace, you deserve the award, not us. You should have it.' She replied, 'Give it to me then.' They didn't. She compares the loss to Scorsese's *Raging Bull* and David Lynch's *The Elephant Man* being beaten at the Oscars by *Ordinary People* and Robert Redford.

Duran Duran admitted they 'borrowed' the staircase idea for their live video.

The concert footage was recorded during her eponymous performances at London's Drury Lane and New York's Savoy theatres.

Goude's 'staircase' was a chunky structure designed for Jones to be able to 'rise above' the stage itself. It was a dramatic piece of set design which Grace used to great effect in the live show, especially when casting striking shadows with an accordion during 'La Vie en Rose' and 'I've Seen That Face Before (Libertango)', or leaping from step to step wearing a gorilla suit (complete with yellow tutu and shocking red lipstick) in the opening scene.

Cultural critic Tavia Nyong'o described *A One Man Show* as the 'performance art of the nightclub'.

O is for A ONE MAN SHOW

Arguably, Grace Jones' career defining release was 1982's *A One Man Show*, a bold collection of live performances, music videos and stills. The concert footage showcased Jones' talents, artistic flair and razor-sharp style. Re-released in 1986 to capitalise on the success of the single 'Slave to the Rhythm', the playful, geometric set and costume designs by Goude, and Grace's sharp-edged posturing was splashed all over MTV, becoming some of the most iconic imagery of the 80s. Grace striking a pose on the stairs, holding a fully extended accordion in her hands. Grace as a conical Pinocchio – post-modern, geometric, pop-art colours and shapes stretched on elastic from her face. Even the name, *A One Man Show*, says it all, cementing Jones' place as a living, breathing work of art and the consummate performer. The collection was nominated for a Grammy Award for Best Video Album in 1983.

P is for PULL UP TO THE BUMPER

Legend has it that 'Pull Up to the Bumper' was recorded in 1980 during the *Warm Leatherette* sessions, but was put on hold until the release of *Nightclubbing* as it was considered a bit too R&B for Grace's new musical direction. It's too funky for *Nightclubbing* as well, but it somehow still fits right in to the mish-mash of robotic quirk-funk. 'Pull Up to the Bumper' was co-written by Jones with Kookoo Baya and Dana Manno, making it a little unusual as a lot of her music at this stage was either a cover or written by someone else. It's a funky, sultry, sleazy, cheeky and catchy-as-anything classic, featuring the ultimate in double entendres. 'Pull Up to the Bumper' became one of Grace Jones' biggest singles of all time in the USA, reaching number five on the Billboard R&B chart and number two on the Hot Dance Club Songs chart.

The B-side of the single release was a Prince-level sexy instrumental jam of the track, perfect for any karaoke star moment. It was called 'Peanut Butter' – which didn't really help to divert the obvious sexual connotations …

Music critic Glenn O'Brien described the song as Grace Jones' 'first car radio hit'.

The music video features night-time cityscapes and traffic tail lights in abstract streams.

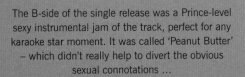

FM 95.5

LCD Soundsystem performed the song with Beth Ditto and her band Gossip at Coachella in 2010.

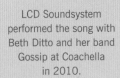

Grace Jones maintains that the song is simply about a 'long black limousine' pulling up alongside a kerb. She said in *Q* magazine as recently as 2008 that the song isn't necessarily about sex. You can picture her knowing wink as she says it, though. It is curious, for someone as outspoken as Jones, that she would deny its true meaning – perhaps she just likes to keep people guessing.

If you're undecided on the meaning or unfamiliar with the lyrics, go and listen again. We'll wait … The chorus lyric referring to '*my* bumper' (rather than '*the* bumper') seals the deal and, really, when have you ever had to 'lubricate' a literal parking space? It became one of her signature tunes and a song that, musically and lyrically, defined the Grace Jones aesthetic in every way.

is also for

Pee-wee's Playhouse
Grace Jones was a guest on the *Pee-wee's Playhouse* 1988 Christmas special. A giant gift box arrives and, before opening it, Pee-wee Herman (played by Paul Reubens) exclaims, 'I hope it's not a fruitcake!' He opens it to reveal an outrageously dressed Grace Jones. She stays on and sings a sultry version of 'The Little Drummer Boy'.

…

Portfolio
Grace Jones' 1977 debut LP was released by Island Records and announced her intention to run for the position of 70s disco nightclub queen. Produced by Tom Moulton, the original version of the LP had side one running the tracks together in a 'disco megamix' format. The three tracks were up-tempo versions of Broadway classics: 'Send in the Clowns', 'What I Did For Love' and 'Tomorrow'.

…

'Private Life'
Jones' cover of The Pretenders track was her first major success in the UK. Taken from her LP *Warm Leatherette*, Jones lent her distinct robotic reggae-funk style to the already reggae-inspired Pretenders version. The track reached 17 in the UK in 1980, and charted again in 1986 as a remix and re-issue single from the *Island Life* compilation.

…

Purple
One of Grace Jones' favourite, and most worn colours. Purple has always been a clear motif throughout her career, both in her stagewear and public appearances: Jones wore head-to-toe purple (including a fur hat and coat) to have dinner at La Vie en Rose in New York in 1987; one of her most iconic Studio 54 photos shows her in a purple batwing bodysuit, and she channeled an Egyptian goddess in a purple headscarf and dripping in gold jewellery on the red carpet for the premiere of *Evita*.

Quelli della calibro 38

Grace contributed two songs to the soundtrack of this 1976 Massimo Dallamano 'poliziotteschi' film (an Italian crime genre popular in the 70s) – 'I'll Find My Way to You' and 'Again and Again'. She also appeared (uncredited) in the film as a club singer.

...

Queens of Disco

Jones was profiled by Graham Norton in this 2007 BBC doco celebrating the queens of the disco era, including Gloria Gaynor, Donna Summer, Chaka Khan and Madonna. Jones does a 'champagne burp' during her interview, like the true queen that she is.

...

Queer icon

In a 2015 profile for *Pitchfork*, journalist Barry Walters examined the queer history of Grace Jones and especially the impact she had on him as a young gay man living in New York in the 80s, 'That night, Grace Jones sang "I Need a Man" just like a man might – tough and lusty, she was a woman who was not just singing *to* them, but also *for* them, *as* them. She was as queer as a relatively straight person could get.'

...

Queen Bitch Jungle Mother of New York

In 2006, Jones was invited to a Delta Airlines party where she allegedly started removing her clothing and proclaiming that she was the 'Queen Bitch Jungle Mother of New York'. Her publicist denies the incident.

'People always like to make me seem taller than I am.' – *Dazed*

'Music has it's own depths, and I let it take me where it takes me. Even if it means stripping all my clothes off.' – *Los Angeles Times*

'I'm always rebelling. I don't think I'll ever stop.' – *The New York Times*

'The Concorde made life a lot easier, and I was the symbol of a Concorde crowd that had replaced the jet set. I flew on the Concorde so many times I knew the pilots. I knew their families. I could have flown the plane, except I would have wanted to do it naked, sprayed silver, in roller skates.' – *I'll Never Write My Memoirs*

'There's a lot of that around at the moment: "Be like Sasha Fierce. Be like Miley Cyrus. Be like Rihanna. Be like Lady Gaga. Be like Rita Ora and Sia. Be like Madonna." I cannot be like them – except to the extent that they are already being like me.' – *I'll Never Write My Memoirs*

'I was skinny as a rail and had high cheekbones and a very interesting face. Or so I was told.' – *Los Angeles Times*

'Shock always sells. You know? But you could shock in good taste.' – *I'll Never Write My Memoirs*

'I've turned down millions of dollars to go on reality TV. It's an absolute no go.' – *BBC News*

is for
QUOTES

Outspoken and whip-smart, unafraid to ruffle feathers, break down barriers or be percieved as a mouthy maverick – Grace Jones can be taken as a spokeswoman for the experimental, the dispossessed, the LGBTQI community, anyone living on the fringes and just about anyone who doesn't slot jigsaw-like into the conservative agenda. But don't look to her to support your cause – while she's outspoken about racism and sexism and discrimination in general, Grace is firmly her own entity who believes very strongly in free speech (in an interview with Susie Stillwell for *Houston Style Magazine*, she compares political correctness with facism, as being 'the complete opposite of freedom'). Witty, acerbic, straight to the point, Grace Jones is eminently quotable because she's never been afraid to say exactly what's on her mind.

R is for

THE RUSSELL HARTY SHOW

One of Grace Jones' more notorious incidents involves her 1980 appearance on the BBC's *The Russell Harty Show*. The strange interview format had Harty (sitting on a swivel chair) speaking to Jones for just a few minutes before introducing his second guest, photographer Patrick Lichfield, then essentially turning away from Grace to talk to Lichfield for a good ten minutes or so, before introducing and speaking to a third guest, photographer Walter Poucher, leaving Grace ignored and clearly bored out of her mind with nothing to do on the other side of him. Grace asked him a few times not to turn his back on her and eventually she got tired of it, and, after threatening to leave the stage, landed a barrage of slaps on the hapless host. What was seen as a prize hissy fit has been greatly exaggerated. Kittenish swipes to Harty's shoulder followed by the pout of a petulant child, everything borders on being playful and humorous and Harty took it in his stride. He moved his chair back slightly to accommodate Jones, the interview went on and Jones even performed a killer version of Roxy Music's 'Love is the Drug,' at the end of the show, removing her oversized coat to reveal a contoured armour-like bustier.

The slapping looks a bit diva-ish out of context, but Jones had to put up with condescending and even slightly racist questions from Harty, who should have known better. Jones said she felt like she was, 'being treated like the hired help', and that when he turned his back on her she started to see her overbearing step-grandfather Mas P.

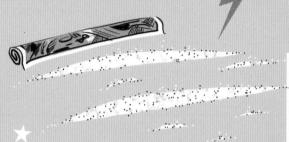

Jones explains the incident in *I'll Never Write My Memoirs*. She says that her sinuses were blocked, she was 'covered in pigeon shit' (possibly referring to being near Trafalgar Square, although the live performance shows a lot of Grace Jones but not a lot of pigeon shit). She also says someone had given her 'bad coke', and her wild eyes and clipped answers certainly back this up. She also admits during the interview, 'I haven't slept in three days.'

Grace has many legendary TV appearances under her belt, being just as fabulous, but not as fiery. She had a great rapport with Joan Rivers, who interviewed her a number of times (it helps that Rivers actually speaks to her like a person rather than treating her like an exotic animal). In 1985 Johnny Carson quizzed Jones on his show about the slapping incident and they share a good laugh.

Racism
Jones has spoken openly on many occasions about being subjected to racism, especially while she was trying to break into modelling and in her early years in America. In *I'll Never Write My memoirs*, co-written by Paul Morley, she reveals that she used to get arrested almost every day in Philadelphia when walking with her boyfriend Sam. She was arrested for prostitution, as that was apparently the only reason a black woman would be walking with a white man. 'They were so racist on both sides—the black cops were just as likely to pick me up and give me a hard time. It became harassment.'

...

Rocky IV
As soon as Dolph Lundgren became a star, the writing was on the wall for Jones' relationship with the hulking, athletic Swede. On the release of *Rocky IV* and his break-out role as Ivan Drago, Lundgren said, 'I walked in to a Westwood movie theater as Grace Jones' boyfriend and walked out ninety minutes later as the movie star Dolph Lundgren.'

...

Joan Rivers
Like Jones, Joan Rivers was a feminist maverick and rabble-rouser. The two clearly got along well, with Rivers interviewing Jones a number of times throughout her career, on both *The Joan Rivers Show* and *The Tonight Show*. When Grace was promoting *Conan the Destroyer*, Rivers hilariously refers to the film as 'Conan the Decorator'.

...

Barry Reynolds
Marianne Faithfull's long time guitarist, Lancashire-born Barry Reynolds was brought in by Chris Blackwell of Island Records to play in Grace Jones' 80s backing band, the Compass Point All Stars. He played guitar on *Warm Leatherette*, *Nightclubbing* and *Living My Life*.

When Russell Harty died, Grace Jones quipped, 'I didn't kill him. I had nothing to do with it. I wasn't there at all. I had an alibi.'

R.I.P RUSSELL HARTY

While Grace is clearly out of sorts during the interview, Harty and guest Patrick Lichfield start rudely mocking Grace, making jokes at her expense, and talking about her as if she wasn't even there. All entirely slap-worthy offences.

Jones said '... they tried to get me back on the show! The ratings soared. I had done him a favour. They wanted a rematch. It was all so tacky.'

In her memoir, Jones said about her behaviour, 'I am being sensitive rather than unruly. In fact, because I was tired and disorientated, everything was heightened. I never wanted to do these kinds of shows high. If anything, I get high afterward.'

S
is also for

Studio 54
The iconic 70s disco at 254 West 54th Street played host to many celebrities, parties and legendary events. Jones was certainly a regular and was often seen there with Andy Warhol, Truman Capote and Divine.

...

Chris Stanley
The swaggering supremo of Jamaica's Music Mountain Studio did a duet with Jones on the song 'Don't Cry Freedom'. The track was from the CD version of her 1989 album *Bulletproof Heart*, which would be her last for 19 years. Stanley co-produced the album with Jones and the pair wrote most of the songs. The two became romantically linked. Some even say they were married – making Stanley her first husband. Jones denies this, however, saying in her memoir that they were never married.

...

Shaved head
When Grace Jones moved to New York to become a model she felt that she needed an extreme look to sell herself. So she shaved off all of her hair. She thought it made her look confrontational and at the same time 'not tied to any specific race or sex or tribe'. She also claims that shaving her head directly led to her first orgasm, 'This is because I am fairly sure the man I had my first orgasm with was Andre, my hairdresser.'

...

Steel Vagina
In the film *Boomerang*, Jones' character Helen Strangé has to come up with a list of names for the company's new perfume. When listing disturbing names including 'Pig Puke' and 'Afterbirth', Eddie Murphy's character, Marcus Graham, has trouble understanding her and thinks she says 'After Bath'. Strangé then reads out 'Steel Vagina'. She says to Graham, 'You understand that one...'

The song that is titled 'Slave to the Rhythm' on the album is not actually the well-known single. The hit track was 'Ladies and Gentlemen, Miss Grace Jones'. It became generally known as 'Slave to the Rhythm' and was written that way in the charts. It was also named 'Slave to the Rhythm' on the Grace Jones best-of album, *Island Life*.

The album cover features yet another memorable and iconic Grace Jones image. Jean-Paul Goude created the image as a photo collage that elongates Jones' hair and open mouth. The creation of the image is shown in the opening of the 'Slave to the Rhythm' music video, along with more of Goude's iconic work.

Grace Jones performed 'Slave to the Rhythm' at Queen Elizabeth II's Diamond Jubilee Concert in 2012. Jones hula-hooped throughout the entire song. The hoop didn't drop once. Try hula-hooping, let alone singing at the same time. She was 64 at the time.

Slave to the Rhythm was produced by ZTT Records supremo Trevor Horn, one of the masters of 80s production (and lead singer of The Buggles). Horn co-wrote much of the material alongside a crack songwriting team that included Bruce Woolley and Stephen Lipson.

The album features some serious music heavyweights, including Glenn Gregory from Heaven 17, pianist Andy Richards, some guitar from Pink Floyd's David Gilmour and an excerpt from an interview with music journalist Paul Morley (also from Art of Noise).

Shirley Bassey opened her 1996 cover album, *The Show Must Go On*, with her version of 'Slave to the Rhythm'.

The song 'Slave to the Rhythm' was written and intended for Frankie Goes to Hollywood as the follow-up to 'Relax'. They went with 'Two Tribes' instead.

S is for

SLAVE TO THE RHYTHM

The seventh studio album from Grace Jones came after a short hiatus from recording. Jones wanted to concentrate on her acting career after the release of 1982's *Living My Life*. When she did come back, it couldn't have been a more dramatic return. Subtitled 'A Biography', *Slave to the Rhythm* is a concept album featuring stories from Jones' life. It includes linked spoken-word pieces between each song, voiced by Ian McShane. Each track is melodically and thematically linked, varied versions of the same song. The album was a hit, breaking into the top 10 in four countries and the top 20 in many more. The titular single was a massive hit for Jones, reaching at least the top 20 in most countries and top 10 in New Zealand, Belgium and Germany. It hit number one on the US Hot Dance Club chart. Over the years, 'Slave to the Rhythm' has become Grace Jones' biggest selling single and one of her most identifiable songs.

is for

TIGER

Tiger print, tiger stripes, tiger growls and tiger prowls ... the one member of the animal kingdom that somehow sums up Grace Jones is the tiger. She name-checks a few other beasts in the song 'Shenanigans', for sure – the cobra, a spider, but she wants to 'swing like a tiger'. She famously posed for *Playboy Italia* in 1978 wearing a tiger-stripe bodysuit, snarling languorously from a leopard-print couch. In the same year she performed at New York's Roseland Ballroom with a live tiger on stage (Grace dressed in tiger stripes and shimmying a long tail), the stage lights going out as she opens the cage door. And of course, whenever she needs to, Grace will pull out the tiger claws and the tiger growl – her trademarks.

For his book *Jungle Fever*, Goude infamously shot Jones prowling like a tiger surrounded by piles of raw meat, under a sign that reads 'DO NOT FEED THE ANIMAL'. The image is still considered controversial – a white man depicting a naked black woman in a cage – and was called out as racist at the time. Goude told the *New York Post* that the image represents 'the tigress image that had been hers since she started singing'.

When quizzed about the 'casting couch' and the #metoo phenomenon, Jones replied, 'A lot of women were put into that situation, but I was a tiger. GRRRAAAAH!'

Tricky
Grace Jones collaborated briefly with the UK trip-hop legend. They made two tracks together, released in 1998 – the up-tempo, almost drum-and-bass track 'Clandestine Affair' and 'Hurricane (Cradle to the Grave)'. Jones and Tricky were apparently working on an album called *Force of Nature* that was shelved due to heated disagreements. 'Clandestine Affair' has become a rare and sought-after promo single and 'Hurricane' went on to be the title track of Jones' 2008 album.

...

Sven-Ole Thorsen
Jones started dating the Danish stuntman and actor (and winner of Denmark's Strongest Man competition in 1983) in 1990. The six-foot-five athlete appeared in many of Arnold Schwarzenegger's movies and made a name for himself as an action hero. Jones and Thorsen have apparently been in an open relationship since 2007.

...

Topless
Always one to embrace nudity, Jones frequently flashes photographers and audiences, and has regularly appeared topless from her early days as a model and throughout the disco era. In 2015, she performed topless at Vivid Sydney, at Brooklyn's Afropunk festival and at Parklife in the UK, adorned in Keith Haring–styled body paint. Rocking up two hours late to a Barnes and Noble book signing for *I'll Never Write My Memoirs*, Jones placated the crowd and photographers by poking out her tongue and lifting up her top.

While there are certainly questions to be raised about Goude depicting Jones as animalistic and primitive, Grace herself told *Paper* magazine, 'It wasn't racist at all. It was him basically putting me on a pedestal.'

Questions surrounding the way Goude exoticised Jones' body were raised again in 2014 when Goude famously used Kim Kardashian to recreate some of his *Jungle Fever* images for *Paper* magazine. The cover featured Kardashian in a clothed version of 'Carolina Beaumont, New York, 1976' (aka 'The Champagne Incident').

Film critic Roger Ebert said of Jones' magnetic screen presence, 'In *Vamp* there is a scene where she crawls toward the camera like a tiger and you'd swear she could finish Conan [the Barbarian] in one bite.'

U
is also for

'Use Me'
Jones covered the Bill Withers track 'Use Me' on *Nightclubbing*, released in 1981. Withers' raspy 1972 funk–soul gem was one of his biggest hits and shared an affinity with Stevie Wonder's 'Superstition', released in the same year. Jones makes the song her own, turning it into a spitting, rolling slice of mechanical space-reggae groove that gives the album more range.

...

Unkle
UK electronic beats outfit Unkle sampled Jones' 'Operattack' from *Slave to the Rhythm* for their track 'Celestial Annihilation'. The song appeared on their 1998 LP *Psyence Fiction*. The original track is a 'Revolution 9'-style experimental a capella wig-out, making it easy for Unkle to nab several sounds and vocal samples and layer them over their dark and moody sci-fi instrumental.

...

Uniforms
Jones' sartorial style is heavily influenced by uniforms, and almost exclusively those worn by men. The pilot's hat and cowl combo she wore on the *Joan Rivers Show* is iconic. In promotional material for her 1978 album *Fame*, she dons a full white naval suit complete with captain's hat in an homage to the classic Marlene Dietrich look. Quite often her outfits would channel religious garb as well, with Greek Orthodox–chic robes and a towering hat.

...

Underwear
When Grace presented namesake Tom Jones with her underthings on stage at the *GQ Men of the Year Awards* in 2012, Tom Jones quipped, 'I didn't think you wore any, to be honest.'

Jones' frequent outspoken behaviour has gotten her into trouble – but it is also why people love her. As she says, 'I can be a pain, but most of all, I can be a pleasure.'

Jones' tour rider was published in her memoir, which included, among the Cristal and Bordeaux, '2 Dozen Findeclare or Colchester Oysters on ice (unopened) – (Grace does her own shucking.)'. Jones swears by oysters to give her energy, and told *The Globe and Mail* that the reason she insists on shucking her own is because, 'There's a pleasure in the ritual.'

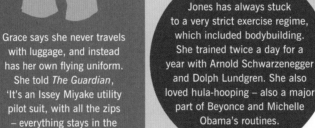

Grace says she never travels with luggage, and instead has her own flying uniform. She told *The Guardian*, 'It's an Issey Miyake utility pilot suit, with all the zips – everything stays in the pockets, my credit card, passport, money ... Whatever I don't have I don't need.'

Jones has always stuck to a very strict exercise regime, which included bodybuilding. She trained twice a day for a year with Arnold Schwarzenegger and Dolph Lundgren. She also loved hula-hooping – also a major part of Beyonce and Michelle Obama's routines.

In *I'll Never Write My Memoirs*, she talks about refusing to go onstage until she was paid. She would say to promoters, 'No, I am not moving until I am paid. I won't even leave the hotel and go to the venue ... give us all your jewelry and watches, your Rolexes, as a deposit. We'll keep them in the safe until I get paid.'

While the requirements of the rider are impressive but relatively standard, the rumours of her tour demands are much more outrageous, including being driven right up to the stage and nightly caviar facials ...

Grace rejects the 'diva' label, saying in her memoir that it's become overused, and worse, implies 'an apparently erratic female whose temperamental qualities, survival instincts, and dedication to perfection are seen as weaknesses, as self-indulgent, not a strength'. She'd prefer to be referred to as 'a Jones'.

is for UNCOMPROMISING

Grace Jones has been called many things: a diva, tough, bold, immovable, immutable and, of course, uncompromising. She has a reputation for being difficult, but Grace is savvy enough to know that's part of her appeal and what has made her such a truly original artist. Jones told *BBC News*, 'I never do what anyone else is doing. I could walk away from music and become a farmer or do some crochet. The worst thing in life for me is to do something I'm not happy doing.' But it hasn't always been easy for Jones. In her memoir, Jones describes her fight for creative control when making the video for 'I'm Not Perfect, But I'm Perfect for You'. 'I had to be a bitch to maintain any kind of authority. Well, if I were a man, I wouldn't have been considered a bitch. If I were a man, I would simply have been in charge, however aggressive and demanding I was.'

V is for VAMPIRE

There was something almost inevitable about Jones' role as Katrina the surreal and artistic stripper vampire in the 1986 Richard Wenk film *Vamp*. Jones the night dweller, disco diva and man eater all in one frightening-yet-sexy format. Her blazing eyes, 'I dare you' stare and perfect cheekbones were tailor-made for the archetypical 80s vampire; a powerful seductress with bite. And her mouth was the perfect vehicle for a set of fangs – when those lips uncurled to show those sharp teeth, it was impossible not to see them as a metaphor for Grace Jones' biting wit and supernatural demeanour. Appearing on *Nightlife* in 1986, host David Brenner introduces her quoting her own words: 'I'm not a freak but I am different. If people think I'm weird, that's ok. It's better than being ignored.' In the interview they laugh about people's misconception that she's a giant, Grace attributing it to the fact that, 'I look people straight in the eyes, so I look like I'm looking right through their souls.'

Grace's nightclub stripper dance scene in *Vamp* steals the film, as does the stunning Keith Haring body paint she reveals as she takes off her clothes.

The film *Vamp* wasn't a huge success. American film critic Roger Ebert gave it a mere two stars, and chalked much of the film's failure to its total waste of Jones, who he described as, 'one of the great undiscovered countries of contemporary entertainment'.

Grace's make-up artist Terry Barber told *The Guardian* in 2010 that, after uncharacteristically appearing during the day for breakfast TV, she said, 'Darling, you're ruining my reputation, you know I'm a vampire.'

Vamp wasn't Jones' only foray into horror. She appeared as Christoph/Christine – a member of a travelling freak show – in the 2001 Canadian/Romanian thriller *Wolfgirl*.

The styling of Grace Jones' character Katrina in *Vamp* was based on Pris in *Blade Runner*, a film that Jones was asked to star in but turned down the role.

Roger Ebert also said, 'Hollywood must know there are a lot of Grace Jones fans. That's why they advertise a movie as if she were the star. Now they should try making a movie where she is the star. Doesn't that seem to be the logical next step?'

It's often been said that Tarantino's *From Dusk Till Dawn* franchise is greatly influenced by *Vamp*. Coincidentally Jones and Tarantino were 'romantically linked' in 2014 when they were seen kissing in a Manhattan nightclub.

V is also for

A View to a Kill
The 14th James Bond film in the series, released in 1985, was the perfect vehicle for Jones. Cast as May Day, the kung fu–kicking, super-strong villain with a sneer to match, Jones made the role her own. Jones also used it as a chance to get then-boyfriend Dolph Lundgren into the movies, although he only had a fleeting role. Despite not having as much screen time as she probably should have, Jones' statuesque form was used on the promotional posters.

...

Video games
Jones lent her dark vocal tones to the character Solene Solux in the video game *Hell: A Cyberpunk Thriller*. Released by GameTek in 1994, *Hell* was a point-and-click adventure set in a distinctly dystopian 2095. The game itself has dated of course, but for its time it was innovative and challenging, not to mention surreal. Jones' character looks vaguely like her, but her dialogue sounds JUST like her. Using one line as an example... 'as for your balls, you obviously haven't been using them either, so they will be mine'. Dennis Hopper also voiced the character Mr Beautiful.

...

Vocal range
Jones is probably mostly thought of as a great performer rather than a classically great singer. She's original and innovative, expressive and experimental. Her vocal range however, tells a different story. She can move from F#1 to C7, a mezzo soprano in opera terms, although by *Bulletproof Heart* she had morphed into a contralto, not bad going.

W
is also for

Andy Warhol
Jones and Warhol partied frequently throughout the 70s and were often seen together at Studio 54. Andy said of Jones, 'You don't get to stay famous for long unless you're always switching. Grace Jones is an example of this.'

...

Whiteface
Jean-Paul Goude produced a series of photographs of Jones painted in whiteface, complete with blue eyes and bright orange hair. One of the images covered *The Face* magazine in 1985. The images are a powerful inversion (and therefore subversion) of the racist blackface used in Hollywood and with groups like the The Black and White Minstrels.

...

Ruby Wax
Grace appeared on *The Ruby Wax Show* in the 90s. Before the interview they do a sketch together. Grace is in the restroom wearing a stunning rainbow sequined bodysuit putting on make up. Wax says to her, 'You look wonderful. You look better than me. Give me some make-up. I'm not going to let you go out looking better than me.'

...

Wolf Girl
This 2001 made-for-tv horror/thriller stars Tim Curry and Shawn Ashmore (who went on to become Iceman in the *X-Men* movie franchise). The film is about a travelling freakshow and Victoria Sanchez plays a girl with hypertrichosis, a medical condition that leads to excessive hair growth all over the body – hence the 'wolf girl' of the title. Of course, Jones plays Christoph/Christine who is half man, half woman. At one point she sings a song about a 'world of wonders' that awaits at the carnival. She begins with her female side to camera, before spinning to reveal the male side.

The B-side of the 'Private Life' single was a warped reggae cover of 'She's Lost Control' by Joy Division, where Jones turns the lyrics to 'I've lost control'.

love

Jones' version of 'Love is the Drug' failed to chart initially as a single. In 1986 it was remixed and included on the compilation *Island Life*. The more up-tempo version reached number 35 in the UK.

In the liner notes of the Jones compilation album *Private Life: The Compass Point Sessions*, The Pretenders' singer Chrissie Hynde is quoted as saying that the Jones cover was one of her career highlights. 'Like all the other London punks, I wanted to do reggae … When I first heard Grace's version I thought "Now that's how it's supposed to sound!".'

Warm Leatherette's album cover was the first of Jones' to be designed by Jean-Paul Goude. It features a black and white photograph of Jones (pregnant at the time) sitting with her arms crossed, her shoulders accentuated by a padded jacket. It was the first image of Jones that really represented this version of the androgynous performer.

Tom Petty wrote a third verse of 'Breakdown' especially for the Grace Jones version that effectively ends the relationship that the song sets up.

Warm Leatherette was the first of the three albums Grace recorded at the Compass Point Studios in the Bahamas.

Peaking at number 17 in the UK, Grace Jones' version of The Pretenders' 'Private Life' became her first chart entry in the UK, where she remains popular to this day.

WARM is for LEATHERETTE

Warm Leatherette was a turning point for Grace Jones. Her fourth studio LP was released in 1980, right on the cusp of disco turning into New Wave, and punk paving the way for new and experimental approaches to music. The titular track was a cover of The Normal's robotic song about becoming sexually aroused by a car crash (inspired by JG Ballard's novel *Crash*, which was made into a film by David Cronenberg in 1996). Of course, Grace put her own spin on the New-Wave sound, and with the help of Sly and Robbie, she invented a melange of reggae and New Wave that reflected the dub electro of Kraftwerk as much as it did her own mechanical, stylistic delivery. The Pretenders' 'Private Life' became another perfect addition to the album and Roxy Music's 'Love is the Drug' completed a triptych that would go on to inform Jones' sound throughout the early 80s. She wasn't quite there yet, though. A naff cover of Tom Petty's 'Breakdown' took some steam out of the record and Jones herself only had a hand in writing one song, the Bowie-esque space-quirk 'A Rolling Stone'. The album wasn't a huge success, only charting in the US, Australia and the UK, but the template was set and Grace's following album, *Nightclubbing,* would see the ideas percolating on *Warm Leatherette* come to fruition.

is for
X-RATED

For someone so outwardly salacious, explicit and outrageous, you might be forgiven for thinking that the x-rated Grace Jones is fully on show. Her onstage performances ooze sexuality and challenge the boundaries of acceptable conservative behaviour. Her talk show appearances leave little to the imagination and her partying is legendary. Wherever she goes, something is always bound to happen to get people talking and cameras flashing. Even amongst her already overt body of work and the string of indecent anecdotes, there are still some moments that are sure to shock even some of her most ardently open-minded fans. From her drug preferences (and methods of taking them), to her various sexual exploits, Grace Jones has more than her fair share of moments unfit for family consumption – and we wouldn't want it any other way.

According to Grace, back in the heady disco days, Studio 54 had a 'rubber room' with walls that 'could be easily wiped down after all the powdery activity that went on', and a hidey-hole on the next floor that was 'beyond secretive ... a place of secrets and secretions, the in-crowd and inhalations, sucking and snorting'.

Jones gained a reputation as a coke fiend, which she has always upheld was undeserved. According to her memoir, 'Coke was never my drug ... if I had taken as much cocaine as it is rumored, I wouldn't have a nose.' She says she actually prefers to put a rock up her ass, 'Sometimes it might get blown up there, one way or another ... Stick a tiny little rock up your butt and it feels fantastic.'

Jones dabbled with ecstasy. In *I'll Never Write My Memoirs*, she explains, 'I had my very first ecstasy pill in the company of Timothy Leary, which is a bit like flying to the moon with Neil Armstrong.' She claims she would only ever take a half tablet, because moderation is key.

When Jones met Queen Elizabeth II after her incredible hula-hooping performance at the Diamond Jubilee Concert, the Queen was disappointed that Jones had changed from her revealing stagewear into normal clothes. The two shared a private joke and afterwards everyone wanted to know what was so funny. Jones will never tell.

Jones also experimented with LSD. Quite a lot apparently. During an interview with *Dazed* in 2015, after an insect flew past her face she asked, 'Did you see that little bug? ... I can never tell if I'm tripping.' She goes on to extol the virtues of acid, 'LSD gave me a lot of insight and sensitivity about what is happening 360 degrees around me ... it gave me a sixth sense of awareness."

Sexual lyrics have always been part of the Grace Jones *modus operandi* – from the suggestive moments of 'I Need a Man' and 'Pull up to the Bumper', to the more overt 'Sex Drive'; she has never shied away from sexual expression and wholeheartedly embraces her sexual desires. She said, 'I mean, what's wrong with being a sex machine darling? Sex is large, sex is life, sex is larger than life, so it appeals to anyone living, or rather, it should.'

X *is also for*

XTC
In the 80s, the Phillipe Starck–designed Starck Club in Dallas became a popular hangout for celebrities and nightclub tragics alike – it was the first 'mixed' club in the city, one that appealed equally to gay and straight patrons. Unsurprisingly, Grace Jones was there for opening night and often played there (she was dubbed the unofficial matriarch of the club). The club has another claim to fame, as the place where a new drug called MDMA first really took off and cemented itself in party culture, under the name ecstasy or XTC.

...

Xenon
Another of Grace's New York nightclub haunts, Xenon was known for having more of a 'fashion crown' than Studio 54's Hollywood scene – luckily Jones elegantly straddled both. Located at 124 West 43rd Street in Midtown, Xenon was known for its space-futurist interior, including a UFO dubbed 'the Mothership' (created by Douglas Trumbull, the Oscar nominee responsible for the special effects in Steven Spielberg's *Close Encounters of the Third Kind*) that would descend from the ceiling.

...

Xmas
Vogue ran a guide on how to have yourself a very Grace Jones Christmas for 2015, seeking inspiration for 'disco-themed Christmas shopping'. The suggestions included a €3500 Loewe leather jacket, some space-age acetate Acne Studios sunglasses, a Benoît Missolin hat with crystal reflector crescent on top, a Saint Laurent by Hedi Slimane fur coat, high-heeled patent leather boots and a pair of €4950 leather and fur Dolce & Gabbana x Frends headphones encrusted with Swarovski crystals and pearls. Or you could just buy a copy of *Nightclubbing* on vinyl.

Y

is also for

Yoga

You don't get a body like Jones' by accident – actually you might, there's no doubt that genetics were at least partially involved – but when she was modelling she had a strict training and diet regime and while filming throughout the 80s she did weight training, boxing and, of course, yoga. (Although, according to Jones when she lived in hotels in Paris with Jerry Hall, they never ate and stayed model-thin via a Champagne-only diet.) Jones currently maintains her incredible physique with a combination of hula-hooping and yoga.

...

Yellow

While Grace mostly wears dark colours and the occasional head-to-toe purple ensemble, yellow is her go-to colour when she wants to brighten things up. She has often worn a vibrant yellow cowl, and while the background for the album cover of *Nightclubbing* was a muted yellow, the promotional material turned it up to eleven. One of her most striking stage sets featured a panel of yellow lights, accenting her silhouette.

...

Yearbook

Jones' yearbook pictures give a fascinating insight into the times, the 'flattened' afro seems to speak to styles she would later adopt. Jones describes the afro as rebellious as no one else had one at the time, but by today's standards it looks pretty tame for Ms Grace Jones.

Like Jones, Saint Laurent believed that drugs could enhance the creative process. However he clearly didn't share Jones' views on moderation and struggled with many addictions, including cocaine, heroin and Coca-Cola.

Grace and Jerry Hall lived and partied together and undoubtedly made an impression wherever they went. Grace describes being able to wear whatever they wanted, sometimes going out together wearing nothing but glitter or African bones around their necks. 'Our boldness knew no bounds because Paris made us seem like we were always on show.'

Frequent fashion collaborator Azzedine Alaïa would go on to design Jones' costumes for her character May Day in *A View to a Kill*.

Grace has fond remembrances of Yves Saint Laurent. She described to *Numéro* an incident at a concert at the Palace where her expectant crowd had literally torn her clothes off, leaving her naked. She made it to her dressing room, 'Yves, who was waiting for me, covered my chest with the belt of his tuxedo, and tied Loulou de la Falaise's scarf around my waist. And then he threw me back onto the stage, shouting, "Come on, get out there!"'

On modelling, Jones is doubtful that what made her so appealing to Yves Saint Laurent back in the 70s would have the same effect today. She told *The Guardian*, 'I'm glad I'm not doing it now, I'd probably be dead. Everybody's so skinny. Size zero is like the walking dead. Not sexy at all.'

Legendary Parisian DJ Guy Cuevas told music journalist Andy Thomas that Paris nightclubs Nuage, Le Sept and Le Palace were where you would find designers Yves Saint Laurent, Valentino and Kenzo mingling with models, actresses, and artists like Andy Warhol and Francis Bacon. Grace opened Le Palace, performing 'La Vie en Rose' sitting astride a pink Harley. 'At the time, Grace was not the girl she would become ... She was only just beginning. But she was fabulous that night ... Everyone was screaming.'

Y is for YSL

Grace Jones' first modelling jobs were in New York, but it was in Paris where her career really took off. Leaving what she considered to be a racist modelling climate in America, Jones found that Paris emphatically embraced her unique looks. Sharing a flat with supermodel (and fellow creature of the night) Jerry Hall certainly helped, and the two of them quickly became partners in crime. Jones worked for several big-name designers including Kenzo and Montana. She hit the gay clubs with Karl Lagerfeld and Giorgio Armani, and became the particular muse of Azzedine Alaïa, who regularly used her to showcase his striking creations, many of which featured the Jones' signature cowl. In 1977–78 Jones strutted the catwalk for Yves Saint Laurent at a time when he had well and truly cemented his place in Paris as a national treasure and legendary designer. Jones was resplendent in many costumes of varying hues, the perfect canvas for Laurent's more brightly coloured creations (she looked especially good in fiery red).

is for ZULA

In 1982, pre-superstar Arnold Schwarzenegger created a legend in the heroic epic *Conan the Barbarian*, a super-violent, Nietzschean, soft-core classic. In 1984, the decision to try to appeal to a wider audience with a PG rating led to the sequel, *Conan the Destroyer*, being regarded as a campy mess. The one thing director Richard Fleischer definitely got right, though, was casting Grace Jones as warrior thief Zula, a formidable fighting machine with a bloodcurdling scream and a vicious glare that would have Conan himself quaking in his leather codpiece. Ever the Jones fan, legendary film critic Roger Ebert praised the performance, 'She has all the flash and fire of a great rock stage star, and it fits perfectly into her role as Zula, the fierce fighter.' Conan was Jones' first major film role, preceding her 1985 role as May Day in *A View to a Kill*.

According to Arnold Schwarzenegger's autobiography *Total Recall*, Jones spent 18 months training for the shoot and managed to accidentally hospitalise two stuntmen with her fighting stick.

Sven-Ole Thorsen (who Jones started dating in 1990) has roles in both *Conan* films, but playing different parts.

Arnie reportedly complained that Grace Jones was 'too tough' during filming, although there are plenty of behind-the-scenes photos that show them hamming it up together.

Schwarzenegger relates that Jones and co-star former NBA star Wilt Chamberlain were hostile on set, arguing about their blackness (Grace, Jamaican-born, objected to being called African-American; Wilt claiming his wealth and lifestyle were culturally 'white', so there was nothing 'black' about him). Schwarzenegger found the arguments complex and fascinating and assures us that Jones and Chamberlain got along extremely well in the end.

Zula wasn't a character in the original *Conan the Barbarian* books by Robert E Howard, and first appeared in the 1978 Marvel comic created by Roy Thomas, John Buscema and Ernie Chan. In a classic Jones twist, Zula was a man in the comic books.

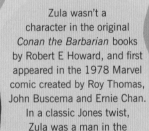

When asked by Olivia d'Abo's Princess Jehnna, 'How do you attract a man?' Zula replies in true Grace Jones fashion, 'Grab him. And take him.'

Although the film garnered mixed reviews, *The Hollywood Reporter* said that Grace was 'the movie's saving grace, her lithe, expressive figure and savage attractiveness making for spontaneity that, at times, appears well nigh incontrollable.'

Z *is also for*

ZTT Records
Zang Tumb Tuum (Fillipino onomatopoeia for a machine gun sound) is a British record label started in 1983 by producer Trevor Horn, *NME* journalist Paul Morley and Horn's wife, famed music businesswoman Jill Sinclair. Over the years the label has featured acts such as Art of Noise, Frankie Goes to Hollywood, 808 State and Grace Jones, and later Seal and The Frames. Jones released one of her most famous records with them, and although Island was still the parent label, Trevor Horn produced *Slave to the Rhythm*. She would work with ZTT again in the 90s for the track 'Let Joy and Innocence Prevail'. Jean Paul Goude was a regular contributor to ZTT album covers.

...

Zebra
Jones opened her 2009 live show at the Hammerstein Ballroom in New York by emerging from a silver obelisk, stepping out to reveal an immaculate zebra-striped catsuit designed by Eiko Ishioka. The look was topped off with a headdress and a flowing silver mane.

...

Zanzibar
Another nightclub where Jones reigned supreme, Zanzibar was located on a dingy street in Newark, New Jersey, and was famous for helping spawn the house sub-genre known as the Jersey Sound. In an interview with *Red Bull Music Academy*, former assistant manager Larkie Rucker recalls Jones cutting her foot at the club and having to be taken to emergency room, 'in the limo in all her glory – makeup and everything. It was seven in the morning, and people were like, "What is this limo pulling up to the emergency room? And who is this woman?"'

Smith Street Books

Published in 2018 by Smith Street Books
Melbourne | Australia
smithstreetbooks.com

ISBN: 978-1-92541880-4

CIP data is available from the National Library of Australia.

Publisher: Paul McNally
Editor: Hannah Koelmeyer
Design: Michelle Mackintosh
Illustration: Babeth Lafon

Printed & bound in China by C&C Offset Printing Co., Ltd.

Book 65
10 9 8 7 6 5 4 3 2 1